The Adventures Of

Nico & Kyra

Responsibility

©2016 Nefretiti A. Morant

Illustrated By Syeda Jabeen Qadri

ISBN-13: 978-1540689719

ISBN-10: 1540689719

1

Dedicated To My beautiful

nieces

Rinniah, Aleah, Layla & Skyla

and my

adorable nephew

Dominic

Table Of Contents

Chapter 1

The summer was passing and Nico and Kyra were enjoying life in Kentsville. They were even excited about starting school in a few weeks. Well maybe not too excited about the school part. They were however looking forward to meeting new friends and having new play dates with these friends.

This Saturday morning would be special. One they would remember for a lifetime. Not that Nico and Kyra knew this as Mom and Dad were waking them up, but this would be a very special day none the less.

"Kyra sweetie." Says Mom as she sits on the edge of Kyra's bed.

"It's time to wake up. Dad and I have a surprise for you." Kyra's eye open. Surprise, Kyra wonders what the surprise could be.

"A surprise?" Asks Kyra sleepily.

"Yes sweetie." Replies Mom.

Kyra sits up in the bed.

"Come on honey, let's go wake up Nico." Says Mom.

Mom and Kyra walk to Nico's room.

"Nico... It's time to wake up." Says Mom.

Kyra jumps on Nico's bed.

"Yeah! Mom and Dad have a surprise for us!" Says Kyra. She was now fully awake and ready for the surprise.

"A surprise?" Asks Nico.

"Yep a surprise." Says Dad as he walks into Nico's room.

"You two jump in the shower, brush
your teeth and head down stairs."
Says Dad.

Mom and Dad walk downstairs and
wait for the children to join them.

Chapter 2

The children loved surprises almost as much as they loved adventures.

After getting dressed Nico and Kyra rush downstairs. They were anxious about their surprise.

"What's the surprise?" Asks Nico as he joins Mom and Dad at the kitchen table.

"If we told you it wouldn't be a surprise." Says Dad.

Nico and Kyra look at each other across the table. They can barely contain themselves. What kind of surprise could Mom and Dad have in store?

"Can we get a hint?" Asks Kyra.

"Nope. A hint may give it away." Says Dad.

"I think they deserve a hint, and I know one that will not give it away." Says Mom.

"You do!" Nico and Kyra say in unison.

"Yes. I do." Says Mom.

"Give us a hint, the suspense is killing me!" Says Kyra.

"This surprise will teach you how to be responsible." Says Mom.

"Responsible?" Asks Nico confused.

"Yep." Mom replies.

The children look at each other. Kyra shrugs her shoulders and shakes her head. The hint had not helped one bit, they had no idea what the surprise could be.

The family finishes up breakfast before heading to the car. They were going downtown Kentsville.

This was the first time that Nico and Kyra had visited downtown. Kentsville's downtown had two or three big buildings, but they were not skyscrapers like the buildings in Capital City.   And there were definitely not as many people on the street.

"This is a small downtown." Says Nico.

"Yes it is, but bigger isn't always better." Says Mom.

Kyra smiles to herself. She wasn't sure if she agreed with Mom. Kyra loved living in a big house as opposed to a small apartment.

"I for one like having a bigger room than I did in Capital City." Says Nico.

"I do too." Says Dad.

"And I love having a big yard!" Adds Kyra.

"I guess some things are better when they are bigger." Says Mom.

"Yeah, not everything. Bigger portions of Kale aren't anything to get excited about. " Says Nico.

The family laughs. Dad parks the car in front of a building with a green awning and a sign that read;

"Animal Shelter." Nico reads the sign out loud.   Kyra reads the sign also. Big smiles spreads across the children's faces.

"Are we getting a dog?" Shouts Kyra. "We'll see , hopefully we'll find one that everyone can agree on." Says Dad.

The family gets out of the car and Nico and Kyra can barely contain themselves as they walk up to the front door of the animal shelter.

Chapter 3

Mom, Dad, Kyra and Nico are greeted by a friendly guy wearing a t-shirt that had the same lettering as the sign out front.

"Well good morning family, my name is Jeff. Hopefully I can help you decide on a pet for your family." He says.

Nico and Kyra smile from ear to ear. They had been asking Mom and Dad for a dog forever.

Jeff leads the family down a long hallway with dogs in kennels on both sides. Nico and Kyra felt sad that they could only get one dog. Especially when there seemed to be so many dogs that needed homes.

"Are we only getting one dog?" Asks Kyra.

"Yes sweetie. We're only getting one dog." Mom replies.

A cute little brown and white dog catches Nioc's attention. The dog runs over to the fence.

"Kyra, come see this one!" Nico shouts excitedly. The dog wags his tail happily. He seems just as eager to see Nico and Kyra as they were to see him.

"Do you like this little guy, his name is Max. He's a Jack Russell Terrier. His owner was an older lady who couldn't care for him anymore. He seems to like you guys as much as ya'll like him." Says Jeff.

"Can we get him Mom?" Ask Nico.

"Yeah Dad can we, can we?" Asks Kyra.

"How old is Max?" Asks Dad.

"Max is three years old. He's house trained, is current on all of his shots and he loves kids." Says Jeff.

Max jumps up and down excitedly.

"Ok boy." Jeff says. "Max seems to really like you two."

"I think we've found our dog says Mom." Mom and Dad smile down at Nico and Kyra.

The family walks back to the front desk with Jeff.

"Ok guys I have some paperwork for your Mom and Dad to fill out, but after that you guys can take your new dog home.   Nico and Kyra liked the sound of that.

Mom and Dad complete the paperwork and soon after Jeff brings Max out on a long orange leash.

"Can I walk the dog to the car?" Asks Kyra.

"Sure." Dad answers.

"I want to walk Max to the car says Nico." He was sad that he had not thought to ask first.

"Kyra asked first, but when we get out of the car you can walk Max in the cul de sac." Dad says.

"How does that sound Nico?" Asks Mom.

"That would be great!" Nico replies. He was happy that he would also get a chance to walk Max.

Mom and Dad finish signing the last adoption papers for Max.

"Congratulations, Max is officially a part of the Culpepper family!" Says Jeff.

The family was all smiles as they left the animal shelter. Everyone was excited to take Max home. Max sat between Nico and Kyra in the back seat of the car.

"Before we head home we are going to stop at the pet store and pick up some stuff for Max." Says Dad.

"Yeah!!!" Reply Nico and Kyra in unison..

Chapter 4

The family pulls up to the pet store. Mom, Dad, Nico and Kyra get out of the car and head inside.   As they walk down the long isles Kyra spots the cutest little doggy collar.

"Can we get Max this pink collar?" Asks Kyra excitedly.

"Pink? Really Kyra.. Max is a boy." Replies Nico.

"So what. Some boys like pink." Says Kyra.

Nico didn't like the idea of his boy dog wearing a pink collar.

Dad kneels down next to Kyra and smiles.

"Why don't we get Max something a little less bright."

"Ok I guess." Kyra replies.

"How about green?" Says Mom.

Mom looks at a green collar with little white bones on it.

"I like it." Nico says.

"Me too." Adds Kyra.

"I guess we've found Max a collar."
Says Dad. Max barks. Nico and
Kyra look at each other and start
laughing.

They pick out a matching green
leash, a doggy bowl, some dog food
and a bed.

"I think we have everything we need
for now." Says Mom.

The family makes their way to the
cash register. Mom and Dad pay for
Max's new things and the family
leaves the store. It was time to take
Max home to his new home.

Mom, Dad, Nico and Kyra ride happily back to their house. Nico and Kyra didn't really know much about taking care of a dog, but they were anxious to learn.

"Guess what Kyra?" Asks Nico.

"What?" Kyra replies.

"This is going to be another great adventure." He answers.

Kyra smiles from ear to ear. Nico was right, having a pet was going to be a another great adventure and

there's nothing Nico and Kyra loved
more than an adventure.

Chapter 5

The family pulls up to their house. As dad reverses into the driveway, Max starts barking. Nico and Kyra can't help but smile.

"Instead of walking Max in the cul des sac can both Kyra and I take Max in the backyard to play?" Asks Nico.

"Yes, but I hope that you guys understand that having a pet is a big responsibility. Before you take Max to play why don't you make sure that he isn't thirsty. There's more to having a dog than just playing." Says Dad.

"Yes Dad." Nico and Kyra reply.

 "Come on Max." Nico says as he turns and heads into the kitchen.

Kyra and Max follow while Mom walks behind them.

"Here you go." Mom says as she helps Nico and Kyra pour out the dog food.

"I'll help you guys set everything up this time, but eventually taking care of

Max is going to be your
responsibility." Says Mom.

Mom helps them put water in one
of the doggy bowls.

Nico and Kyra watch and try to
remember everything that Mom and
Dad was showing them.   They
wanted to take good care of Max. It
seemed easy enough. Taking care of
Max even seemed like it would be
fun.

Max happily eats his food and drinks
some of the water. Nico and Kyra
could tell that he was happy because

his tail whipped back and forth quickly.   Max looks up from his bowl and barks. He was ready to play. Nico and Kyra were ready to play also.

"Can we go in the yard now?" Kyra asks.

"Yes, you guys can go on out but make sure you take the dog poop bags." Says Dad.

"The WHAT!" Say Nico and Kyra as they look at each other incredulously.

"The dog poop bags is what you will to clean up after Max if he goes to the bathroom." Says Dad.

"Don't worry I'll help this first time." Says Dad.

"Ok, I'll call you guys in for lunch in an hour." Says Mom.   Nico, Kyra and Max run outside.   Dad heads outside with Nico and Kyra.

Nico finds a stick and he picks it up. Max runs happily to his side.

"I think he want's to play catch." Says Kyra.

Nico throws the stick across the yard and Max runs after it. Max excitedly picks up the stick with his mouth and runs back over to Nico.

"Wow, he's really good at this." Says Kyra.

Soon Max walks over to a tree and begins to scoot his bottom down to the ground.

"I think Max is going guys. Time to pick up the poop." Dad Says.

Dad shows Nico and Kyra how to pick up Max's poop and tie off the bag.   Dad takes the dog poop bag inside and Nico and Kyra continue to play with Max. Before they knew it Mom was calling them inside. They were having so much fun that Kyra and Nico didn't even think about the time traveling bench.

They were also very surprised when mom called them in for lunch. Had it really been an hour? The three of them run into the house for lunch.

Nico and Kyra rush to wash their hands. They were hungry and ready to eat. They both sit at the table as Mom sets her famous nachos salad on the table.

"I can't wait to get to the nucleus." Says Nico. Nico and Kyra called the center of the salad the nucleus because it always seemed to have the most meat and cheese.

"Hold up... what about Max? Neither of you checked to make sure that Max's bowl is full. He was outside playing too.   Maybe he's thirsty or hungry." Says Mom.

"Oh he can have some of my nachos. Here boy." Nico says as he motions for Max to come to him.

"Good thinking dude." Adds Kyra.

"Hold up, you can't feed dogs people food.   It can be dangerous for them." Says Mom.

Nico and Kyra look at each other, they were confused.

"What's the big deal, we eat people food all the time." Says Kyra.

"Human food can cause pancreatitis in dogs." Says Dad.

"Pancrea... what?" Says Nico.

"Pancreatitis is what happens to your pancreas when it is swollen. When this happens your body no longer gets the nutrients it needs from the food that you are eating." Says Dad.

"Oh my goodness! I don't want Max to get that!" Exclaims Kyra with a worried look on her face.

"Me neither... Pancreatitis sounds horrible!" Adds Nico.

"Well in that case you need to get up and fill Max's bowls with some food and water." Says Mom.

"Ok, got it." Says Nico.

"Me too! Nico, you get the food, I'll handle the water." Says Kyra.

Max barks at the children.

"Guess he doesn't want pancreatitis either." Says Nico. The whole family busts out laughing.

"You kids are too much." Says Mom as she shakes her head.

"I'm telling you guys, taking care of Max is a big responsibility. You always have to make sure that Max is taken care of. Do you guys understand?" Asks Dad.

"Yes Dad." Nico and Kyra say in unison.

Nico and Kyra refill Max's water and food bowl.

"I'm so happy that we have Max." Says Kyra.

"Me too." Says Nico.

Max barks and walks over to his bowls.   He eats some of his dog food and drinks all of the water.

"I guess he was thirsty." Says Kyra.

The children walk over to the table and sit back down.

"I want you guys to know that you are doing a great job taking care of Max." Says Mom.

"Thanks Mom!" They say in unison. They grin from ear to ear. They wanted to be responsible dog owners.

The family blesses the food before eating. Nico and Kyra felt very happy that Max was now apart of their family. As far as Nico and

Kyra were concerned the move to Kentsville was getting better and better everyday.

Chapter 6

After lunch Nico and Kyra wanted to go upstairs and play. As they stand and begin to run up the stairs Mom calls after them.

"Before you guys go upstairs, I think you should take Max for a walk. "

"A walk. But we were just outside playing and he ran around the whole time." Whined Nico.

"Yeah." Added Kyra. The children wanted to go play in their rooms. Nico wanted to play video

games and Kyra wanted to play with
her dolls.

"Well he will need one more walk
before the night is out. You guys can
go play for a little while, but once
Max gets antsy we will take him for a
walk." Says Mom.

"Ok Mom." Says Kyra. The children
run upstairs and Max follows them.

Kyra begins to play with her dolls
and Nico goes to his room to play
with his video games. The children
were happy to have some time to
themselves. Shortly after they had

begun to play; Max ran downstairs and started barking.

"Nico, Kyra... Max is ready to go outside." Yells Mom.

Nico and Kyra couldn't believe that Max was ready to go outside already.

It felt like they had just come in from the backyard.

"Man Mom and Dad were right, taking care of a dog is a big responsibility." Says Kyra.

"For real!" Says Nico.

"Hey Nico do you think that Max can time travel with us?" Kyra asks.

"I don't know but there's one way to find out." Nico replies. The kids run downstairs and meet Max at the back door. Max barks.

"Ok, ok.. were heading out now." Kyra says to Max. Kyra could not understand why he was so anxious to get outside. It felt like they had just come from outside. Plus Kyra was having fun playing with her Barbie dolls.

Nico opens the door and Max bolts outside.

The children follow Max. He seemed very excited to be outside. Nico and Kyra were starting to understand that being a responsible pet owner meant that they would have to consider Max's needs at all times.

As they throw the ball and Max happily runs to catch it, Nico walks over to the bench. Kyra looks over at him.

Nico sits on the bench and Kyra walks over also. Max notices them and runs over too.

"Come on boy." Says Kyra as she motions for Max to jump on her lap.

Max jumps onto her lap and the backyard begins to fade.

Chapter 7

Nico and Kyra look around, they were anxious to see where the bench had taken them this time. They spotted men and women walking down a wide street. Max begins to bark loudly. Nico and Kyra turn around to the sight of an horse drawn chariot moving quickly towards them.

"Move quickly!" Shouts a young girl standing on the side of the road. In the nick of time Nico, Kyra and Max jump out of the way. The chariot thunders by, and Max barks at it ferociously. Nico and Kyra are grateful for the warning.

"Are you guys ok?" Asks the girl.

"I didn't even realize that the chariot was coming straight at us." Says Nico.

"What are you guys doing in the middle of the Avenue anyway?" Asks the girl. Kyra and Nico look around at the bustling city.

"What is the name of this city?" Asks Kyra.

"This is Meroe. What are your names?" Asks the girl.

"I'm Nico, this is Kyra, and this is our dog Max. What's your name?" Says Nico.

"I'm Niat." Says the girl.

"Meroe?" Asks Kyra.

"Yes island city, land of Iron." Says Niat.

"It is very beautiful here." Says Kyra.

"Since you are new here I will show you all around Meroe. I am on my way to the baths to swim and collect a payment." Says Niat.

"The baths?" Asks Nico.

"Yes, have you never been to one?" Asks Niat.

"No, but we would like to see what it is like." Replies Nico.

"Come, I will show you through the city as we walk to the baths." Says Niat. Max barks and Niat smiles at him.

"That would be great!" Says Kyra.

Chapter 8

The children walk down the street together. The road is smooth and wide. The buildings lining the street are made of smooth clay. Some are enclosed in tall walls. People dressed in white robes like Niat walk in all directions.

"The baths are very popular here. I am heading there now to collect a payment for the iron weapons and tools my father makes."

"Wow your dad makes iron? Asks Kyra.

"Yes he makes the finest Iron in Meroe." Answers Niat.

"In all of Meroe?" Asks Kyra.

"Yes in all of Meroe; land of iron, trade and commerce." Says Niat.

"What else is Meroe known for?" Asks Nico. Niat smiles.

"Why do you smile?" Ask Kyra.

"Because I am surprised that you two have not heard the songs." Answers Niat.

"The songs?" Say Nico and Kyra. They were really confused now.

"Yes the songs of the ships gliding down the cataracts of the Nile. The songs of the young and old tradesmen who venture across the Earth to bring great fortune to their families and Meroe." Niat stops and turns towards them.

"Great are the men of Meroe.. Men both young and old. .. They travel the corners of Nut's dome.. protected by the Goddess... She blesses the sacred

land of Meroe... land of Iron... land of
gold.. land of prosperity......Great is
this land protect within the womb of
Nut.... long live the prosperity of
Meroe.. life and love to Meroe most
sacred of lands..." As her beautiful
voice trails off Max barks.

"Wow Niat your voice is beautiful."
Says Kyra. Kyra loved the song and
Niat had sang it beautifully.

"Yeah your voice is nice Niat, even
Max loves it." Adds Nico.

"Thanks." Says Niat as she smiles
proudly. She liked that song. Her big

brother Seket was one of those brave men. He sailed to Egypt, Abyssinia, Rome, Napata and many more great nations trading the goods of Meroe.

She missed her brother.

"That's really awesome." Says Nico.

"What does awesome mean?" Asks Niat.

"Oh, it means really good." Kyra responds.

"Interesting." Niat replies. She liked Kyra and Nico, Max wasn't too bad either.

The children pass a small group of houses with straw roofs. Nico and Kyra were amazed by the sights and smells of the city. Music is soon added to their experience. As they walk they come across a group of musicians playing the same song Niat had just sung to them.

"Is that the same song?" Ask Krya. "Yes!" Says Niat. "This is it." She replies excitedly.

The children stop to listen to the musicians. Nico and Kyra listen in amazement as the drums and stringed instruments add harmony to the beautiful song Niat was just signing.

"Niat... I think I love Meroe." Says Kyra. Niat smiles.

"Many do Kyra." She replies. Nico starts dancing and people start to gather to watch. Kyra joins him and so does Max.

The song ends and the crowd applauds. Nico and Kyra felt good. They had never heard of Meroe, but they were glad that the magical time traveling bench had brought them here. As the children walk they pass a stall of women cooking meat on a hot stove.

"What is that delicious smell?" Asks Nico.

"That is roasted lamb. The women prepare it with spices and herbs that are grown on the farm estates of Meroe."

"Can we try it?" Asks Kyra.

"I don't see why not." Niat
replies. She looks up at the sky. "I do
have some time. Lets stop for a
treat." She says.

Nico looks up.

"How does looking at the sky let you
know that you have time?" Says Nico.

"Simple. I know that the woman my
father has me meeting will be at the
bath until two hours past noon." Says
Niat.

"How does the sky tell you this?"
Asks Nico.

"Simple, the sun is at it's highest point
in the sky now.   This is how I know
that I will get to the baths before my
father's customer leaves." Says Niat.

I will buy some of the lamb for
you to taste. The children stop at the
food stand. Niat buys lamb for the
three of them.

"How did you get money?" Asks
Nico. He and Kyra didn't have money
or get to walk around their town on
their own.

"The money is my pay." Says Niat.

Kyra and Nico were very impressed by that fact that Niat had what seemed to be a job. Niat didn't seem that much older than them.

"Yes I help my father with the sale transactions of his Iron goods. He smelts weapons, wares and tools for Meroe." Niat replies.

"Oh wow! Are you rich?" Ask Kyra.

Niat smiles. Nico and Kyra were younger than her, but she did not understand why they were so impressed. Many of the children in Meroe were apprentices to their families businesses."

"Do the children not enter into apprenticeships where you are from?" Niat asks.

"The only thing children where we are from do, is go to school and get good grades.

"Interesting." Says Niat. Niat pays for the lamb. The vendor smiles at the children as she hands them each a piece of lamb served with fried cassava chips.

Kyra and Nico were so impressed
with the smell of the food, that they
bite into the lamb immediately. After
the first bite Nico eats his so fast that
he has the sauce from the lamb all
over his face.

"Nico!" Says Kyra as she motions to
his face.

"What Kyra?....This is soo good!" He
says as he finishes off the chips.

"Your face man... You have lamb
juice all over it."

"Oh!" Says Nico sheepishly. He feels slightly embarrassed as he wipes his mouth with the back of his hand.

"Here, use this." Says Niat as she hands him a cloth.

"But it's so clean, I'll ruin it." Says Nico. He didn't want to make Niat 's cloth dirty.

"Oh go ahead Nico. I rather you use the cloth than walk around looking like a hyena." She says.

"A hyena!" Say Nico and Kyra in unison. They had never heard of anyone being referred to as a hyena. The three children begin laughing so hard that a lady walking past stops to smile at them.

"Well aren't you children full of happiness. Must be nice." She says.

"That lamb was the most delicious thing that I have ever tasted. I'm one full hyena." Says Nico as he pats his belly. The three children look at each other and begin laughing again. Max must have felt like being included too, because he begins to bark excitedly.

"You want some boy?" Asks Nico.

"Remember what Mom said Nico."
Says Kyra.

"Oh yeah the pancreatitis thing. Sorry
boy, your going to have to wait until
we get back home." Says Nico as he
kneels down and rubs the top of Max's
head.

"Yeah boy, it's for your own good."
Says Kyra.

"Come on guys, I have to get to the
baths sooner than later." Says Niat.

Kyra finishes up her meat and they
all follow Niat to the city's royal

baths. Nico and Kyra were ready to continue their adventure.

Chapter 9

As the children approach the royal baths the sights of bright pyramids shine on the horizon.

"I did not know that Meroe had pyramids like Kemet!" Says Nico excitedly.

He remembered the pyramids of Kemet. These pyramids were not as big but there were so many more of them and their outlines were a bright reminder of the beautiful architecture he had seen in Kemet.

"So you have been to Kemet?" Asks Niat. She was surprised that Nico and Kyra had traveled to Kemet. They seemed very young to have traveled so far.

"Yes we have, and Kemet is almost as beautiful as Meroe." Replies Kyra.

"Why thank you." Says Niat.

We are here, these are the baths

Chapter 10

The children walk into a large stone building. Nico and Kyra were immediately impressed with the high arched ceiling.

"This is incredible." Says Kyra as she looks up into the domed ceiling. she had never seen anything like it.

"Come on the hour is getting away from us." Says Niat.

Nico and Kyra follow Niat down a corridor that opens up into a room with a large pool. Men and women sit in and around the pool.

 "This is soo cool!" Exclaims Nico.

"The water is actually warm." Says Niat.

"Kyra and Nico look at each other as they realize that Niat did not understand what Nico meant.

"No cool means, good or nice." Kyra says to Niat.

"Ahh… I see." Says Niat.   There's the lady I am meeting, you two wait here.

"Can we go for a swim?" Asks Nico.

"Yes. First I must take care of my responsibilities. " Niat replies.

"I guess we aren't the only ones with responsibilities." Kyra says to Nico.

"I know right. Do you think kids always had responsibilities." Nico asks Kyra.

"Nico, I think kids have had responsibilities for as long as they've had parents." Kyra replies.

"I guess that means kids have always had it tough." Nico replies. The two begin laughing.

Niat walks over to the Nico and Kyra after she returns from making her transaction.

"Come on, we can go swimming now." She says.

The three swim and play in Meroe's bath house. It was great fun and even Max seemed to be a natural, as he doggy paddled around.

After a few hours of swimming and playing Niat says;

 "This is fun, but I must get going. It is getting late and my mother will be looking for me to help her with dinner."

"Wow, you sure have a lot of responsibilities." Says Nico.

"You are right Nico, but these responsibilities will prepare me for life as an adult." Niat replies with a smile.

"Niat I think that you are absolutely right." Kyra says.

"Yeah Niat you are going to be one heck of an adult." Nico adds with a smirk.

The children all laugh and Max barks.

"Thank you guys." Niat says.

Max barks and Nico and Kyra remember that it was probably time for him to eat.

"We have to go take care of our responsibilities too." Says Nico.

"Yeah Max is probably hungry. Right boy." Kyra says as she bends down to rub his neck.

Max barks and Kyra and Nico smile at him.

"It was nice meeting you two." Says Niat.

"It was great meeting you as well Niat. Thank you for showing us around Meroe " Says Kyra.

The children hug each other and say their goodbyes. Niat heads to her home and Nico turns to Kyra.

"Are you ready to go home?" He asks.

"Yep, I sure am. I can't wait to ask Mom and Dad if they've ever heard of Meroe." Says Kyra.

Nico picks up Max and Kyra puts her hand on Nico's shoulder.

"I sure wish we were back home." The two say in unison. The land of Meroe fades into sandy green bits and suddenly Nico and Kyra are back in their backyard sitting on their time traveling bench.

"Whoa!" Says Nico. Max barks and Kyra laughs.

"You two are a mess. Come on let's go ask Mom and Dad if they've ever heard of Meroe." Says Kyra excitedly.

Nico and Kyra run inside and Max follows.

Chapter 11

Kyra, Nico, and Max run through the backyard and into the house.   They kick off their shoes and head into the family room. Mom and Dad were sitting quietly reading.

"Mom, Dad have you ever heard of Meroe." Asks Nico.

"Yes I have." Mom replies.

"You have?" Asks Dad.

"Yes there was a special on T.V about Meroe a few months ago." Mom replies.

"There was!" Ask Nico and Kyra in unison.

"Yep, there sure was. They talked about how Egypt is known for its pyramids, but Meroe has way more pyramids than Egypt." Mom says. Nico and Kyra couldn't believe that

Mom knew about Meroe.

"What else do you know about Meroe?" Asks Kyra.

"Well they were known for trading all over the ancient world. They even had courts and baths houses for Meroe's rich citizens." Mom says.

"Wow that is so cool." Says Nico.

"Sure is." Dad says.   Max barks.

"I guess it's time to feed Max." Says Nico.

"You guys are handling your responsibilities, quiet well." Says Mom.

"Thanks Mom. You know Mom that these responsibilities will help prepare us to be good adults!"

Says Nico.

Dad and Mom look at each other in surprise. They were impressed by how responsible Nico and Kyra were becoming.

"Come on Kyra lets go get Max something to eat and drink." Says Nico.

Nico, Kyra and Max leave the family room.   They were pet owners now and taking care of Max meant being responsible. Nico and Kyra were ready to be the responsible pet

owners that Mom and Dad expected
them to be.

Some Fun Facts About Meroe

Meroe was a city in the southern part of the Kingdom of Kush. Meroe was the capital city and was known for it numerous pyramids. Meroe existed from .800 BCE to approximately 350 CE.

The Kings and Queens of Kush are buried in Meroe.

The culture flourished during Kemet's twenty fifth dynasty. The importance of the city increased in 280 BCE when the royal burial ground was transferred from the Kushite city of Napata to the Kushite city of Meroe.

During the fifth century BCE, Greek historian Herodotus described it as "a great city...said to be the mother cities."

Meroe was located along the middle Nile which served it well in the production and trade of pottery, iron and many other goods. For centuries the pyramids which lined the skyline of Meroe stood as a testament of culture, modern innovation, and

grandeur to those who visited her
lovely shores.

Thank You for reading The Adventures of Nico & Kyra. To follow more of their adventures please ask your parents if you can visit their website and social media pages.

https://nicokyra.com/

Made in the USA
Columbia, SC
19 November 2024

46974344R00054